Daily Life

The Oregon Trail

Dana Meachen Rau

KidHaven Press

KidHaven Press, an imprint of Gale Group, Inc.
10911 Technology Place, San Diego, CA 92127

Dedication

For Chris, who loves to teach American history, and for Charlie and Allison, who make every journey an adventure.

Library of Congress Cataloging-in-Publication Data

Rau, Dana Meachen, 1971–
The Oregon Trail / by Dana Meachen Rau.
    p. cm. — (Daily life)
    Includes bibliographical references (p.   )and index.
    ISBN 0-7377-0539-6 (hardback : alk. paper)
    Summary: Discusses the westward migration of settlers along the Oregon Trail and describes the equipment and supplies necessary for the journey, what a typical day on the trail was like, the dangers the travelers faced, and the hope which helped them reach Oregon Country.
    1. Oregon National Historic Trail—History—Juvenile literature. 2. Frontier and pioneer life—Oregon National Historic Trail—Juvenile literature. 3. Pioneers—Oregon National Historic Trail—History—Juvenile literature. 4. Pioneers—Oregon National Historic Trail—Social life and customs—Juvenile literature. 5. Frontier and pioneer life—West (U.S.)—Juvenile literature. 6. Overland journeys to the Pacific—Juvenile literature. [1. Oregon National Historic Trail. 2. Frontier and pioneer life—West (U.S.) 3. Pioneers. 4. Overland journeys to the Pacific. 5. West (U.S.)—Social life and customs.] I. Title. II. Series.
    F597 .R26 2002
    917.804'22—dc21

    2001001440

Printed in the U.S.A.

Contents

Chapter One
Supplying the Prairie Schooner   4

Chapter Two
A Day on the Dusty Trail   13

Chapter Three
Dangers and Death   20

Chapter Four
Keeping Hope   27

Notes   40

Glossary   42

For Further Exploration   43

Index   45

Picture Credits   48

Chapter One

Supplying the Prairie Schooner

Between 1840 and 1860, nearly 250,000 people packed up their lives into canvas-covered wagons and traveled westward across America on the Oregon Trail. The route led to Oregon Country—the half-million square miles of undeveloped territory that includes the present-day states of Oregon, Washington, and Idaho and parts of Canada. The move westward began with mapmakers and explorers and grew to include entire families. In 1843, the year known as the Great Migration, more than 1,000 people made the trip in a single wagon train.

Families had many reasons for walking and riding wagons across the vast and dangerous lands of America. Many Americans lost a lot of money following the Panic of 1837, when banks failed and many farms and other businesses went bankrupt. Farmers, especially in the Midwest, looked to the West for a fresh start. Other people wanted to leave the East because they strongly

The wagon train of the Great Migration stretched for miles.

opposed slavery. They wanted to settle in a land where slavery was not practiced. Some travelers were missionaries who wanted to spread Christianity to American Indians.

The Route

The Oregon Trail is sometimes called the Oregon-California Trail, because travelers heading to Utah and California took part of the same route as those heading to Oregon. The most common **jumping-off spots** were Independence and St. Joseph, Missouri, and Council Bluffs, Iowa.

People followed rivers when they could to be as near as possible to a source of fresh water. First, wagons traveled up the Kansas River to the Big Blue River until it met the North Platte River. Travelers followed the North Platte across the dry and dusty Great Plains. They often stopped at Fort Laramie and Independence Rock. At this point, they reached the Sweetwater River.

Next, they crossed the Rocky Mountains over the South Pass, then moved on to Fort Hall on the Snake River. At this point, the travelers decided to head north to Oregon or south to Utah and California.

After crossing the Snake River, travelers going to Oregon walked along the river's bleak plains. Next, they

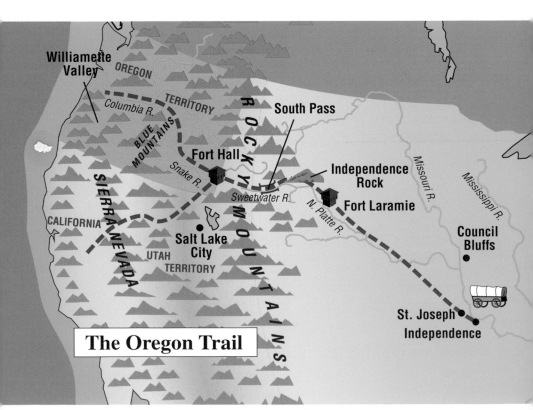

The Oregon Trail

struggled across the Blue Mountains to Oregon. Here, they could take the Columbia River or the Barlow Road to reach the rich farmland of the Willamette Valley.

The Start of a Long Journey

The journey began in towns along the Missouri River where people gathered to buy supplies, meet fellow travelers, organize wagon trains, and hire guides. These towns were easily reached by the Midwestern farm families who made up most of the settlers. The trail led from jumping-off spots to the water route across the West. The journey covered about two thousand miles and took travelers about six months. Today, airplane passengers make the same journey in less than four hours.

A seven-year-old boy named Jesse A. Applegate made the journey in 1843. Later in his life, he described his feelings about the long trip:

> How little we guessed of what the future held in store for those wagons of courageous people. Little did we dream of the weary days and weeks and months of that long and toilsome march towards the land of the setting sun, a test of courage of soul.[1]

Independence, Missouri, was one of the most popular jumping-off spots. Travelers camped in tents outside of town, and went in during the day to stock up for the trip. A family needed between $500 and $1,000 to buy the necessary supplies.

A wagon was the most expensive and important supply. Some people already owned one, but many chose to begin the trip with a new vehicle. Sturdy wagons could hold up to two thousand five hundred pounds. Canvas stretched over bows of wood covered the wagon and helped keep out rain and dust. Because the covers made the wagons look like sailing ships, or **schooners**, the wagons became known as "prairie schooners." Most often, a single wagon held one family and all of its supplies. A young man traveling alone might hire himself out to a family, exchanging his labor on the journey for food and the shelter of the wagon.

Next, a family needed about four to six animals to pull the wagon. Most chose oxen. Oxen ate grass along the way, so the travelers did not have to bring extra food for them. Some people chose mules because they walked faster—but mules were not as strong. Peter Burnett wrote why he chose oxen:

> The ox is a most noble animal, patient, thrifty, durable, gentle and does not run off. Those who come to this country will be in love with their oxen. The ox will plunge through mud, swim over streams, dive into thickets and he will eat almost anything.[2]

Some families also bought a few saddled horses for riding and a cow or two for milking along the way.

Supplies for the Long Trip

Families needed to purchase enough food from stores in town to last the whole journey. They could not bring anything that had to stay cold or that would spoil, such as fresh fruits and vegetables. Most food consisted of

The covered wagon was home on the long trip west.

bulk dry goods, which sometimes weighed more than one thousand pounds. In 1845, Joel Palmer recorded in his journal what he bought to eat on the trail:

> 200 pounds of flour,
> 300 pounds of pilot bread,
> 75 pounds of bacon,
> 10 pounds of rice,
> 5 pounds of coffee,
> 2 pounds of tea,
> 25 pounds of sugar,
> a half-bushel of dried beans,
> 1 bushel of dried fruit,
> 10 pounds of salt,
> a half-bushel of cornmeal,
> and a small **keg** of vinegar.[3]

Settlers bought dry goods such as flour and sugar before starting their journey.

Food was not the only essential supply. Guns and gunpowder were needed for hunting and protection. Boxes held rope, shovels, chains, and tools to make repairs on the wagon. Most families brought a pot called a Dutch oven, a skillet, plates and cups, knives and forks, a butter churn, and a coffee pot. They filled a trunk with candles, blankets, books, medicine, matches, a bible, and one change of clothes for each person.

Once a wagon was packed, travelers grouped together to form companies. It was much safer to travel in a "wagon train" than it was to travel alone. Choosing travel companions was an important decision. A person with a useful skill and occupation, such as a doctor or a pastor, was desirable. Others were chosen based on the amount of their supplies. Catherine Haun describes how her group was chosen:

> For the common good each party was "sized up" as it were. People insufficiently provisioned or not supplied with guns and ammunition were not desirable but, on the other hand, wagons too heavily loaded might be a hindrance.[4]

Travelers found safety in numbers in a wagon train.

Some very large wagon trains included up to one hundred wagons, with hundreds of people and more than a thousand animals. Well-organized companies chose a leader, or captain, and required members to follow a list of rules. Some companies also hired guides. These were men who had traveled the trail before or Native Americans who knew the land well.

Generally, wagon trains tried to leave the jumping-off towns in May. Leaving sooner meant having to cross the Great Plains before spring rains made enough prairie grass to feed the livestock. Leaving later risked the dangerous possibility of getting caught in the Rocky Mountains in the harsh cold and winds of winter. Depending on the terrain, wagons traveled from five to fifteen miles a day. The travelers knew the next months would be hard and tiring. But their hopes for a new life in Oregon Country urged them onward to an uncertain journey across America.

Chapter Two

A Day on the Dusty Trail

After setting off on the trail, wagons soon reached the plains along the North Platte River, which runs through present-day Nebraska and Wyoming. The wagon train plodded along day after day across this dusty land. One day was much like another, filled with many chores and hours of walking.

The day began at 4 A.M. when the men on night watch fired their rifles, the "alarm clock" that woke the company. Immediately, the camp bustled with activity. The men headed out to gather the cattle that had been let loose to graze all evening.

Women lit fires to cook breakfast, starting them with wood or dried plants. Sometimes, in dry or tree-less areas, they burned spare wagon parts. Along the North Platte River, they used dried buffalo droppings, called **buffalo chips**, as fuel for their fires.

Breakfast was a hearty meal. The previous evening, women may have placed a pot of beans in the campfire ashes, ready in time for the morning meal. The women piled plates high with fried bacon, biscuits, pancakes, or muffins. Everyone drank coffee.

Milking a family's cows was the children's chore. At home, one of their jobs would have been to churn the milk for hours until it became butter. But on the trail, they poured milk into a churn hung high on the side of the wagon. The constant bumping and bouncing of the wagon all day created butter and buttermilk.

By 7 A.M., the wagons were repacked. The blowing of a trumpet or bugle told the wagons it was time to roll. The captain led the train and set the pace. Jesse Applegate wrote of the busy morning:

> From six to seven o'clock is a busy time; breakfast is to be eaten, the tents struck, the wagons loaded and the teams yoked and brought up in readiness to be attached to their respective wagons. All know when, at seven o'clock, the signal to march sounds, those not ready to take their proper places in the line of march must fall into the dusty rear for the day.[5]

Usually, travelers in the rear of the wagon train were coated with dust from head to foot within a few hours. To be fair, the captain divided the company into groups, and rotated the wagons' order every day. But the wagon train did not always travel in a line. On flat, open stretches, the wagons spread out, sometimes as wide as a mile.

Along the Trail

On some days, as the wagons started to roll, the captain sent out a hunting party of ten to fifteen young men in search of game. They returned with birds and small animals. On the prairie, they hunted buffalo, which

Hunters often rode ahead of the wagons to hunt for game such as buffalo.

roamed the plains by the millions. But the mostly inexperienced hunters were not always lucky.

If a lucky shot did bring down a buffalo, the settlers tried to use all its parts, just as the American Indians did. They ate some of the fresh meat and preserved the rest by **jerking**, or drying. They cut the meat into strips and strung the strips on ropes hung on the outside of the wagon cover, where they dried in the sun. They saved the "jerky" for times when the hunters returned empty-handed and food was scarce.

Most people did not ride in the wagons. Families walked, even on rainy days. Walking was actually much more comfortable than riding because the slow wagons jumped and shook on the uneven, rutted trail. Also, the oxen already had a heavy load to carry without having to haul people, too. Only mothers with small babies, the sick, or older people would ride.

At midday, the dusty wagon train came to a halt. It was time for "nooning." Everyone was hot, tired, and ready for a break. Settler Catherine Haun wrote:

> When possible we rested the stock an hour at noon each day; allowing them to graze, if there was anything to graze upon, or in any case they could lie down, which the fagged [exhausted] beasts often preferred to do as they were too tired to eat what we could give them. During the noon hour we refreshed ourselves with cold coffee and a crust of bread. Also a halt of ten minutes each hour was appreciated by all and was never a loss of time.[6]

During the hours of walking, the travelers often encountered Native Americans. Most settlers feared them but very few wagon trains were ever attacked. Many Native Americans followed wagon trains to trade goods. Trading was a traditional and vital part of Indian life. Lydia Allen Rudd wrote in her diary, "July 15 . . . Some of the snake Indians came to our camp this morning I swaped some hard bread with them for some good berries."[7] Jesse Applegate remembers, "Many Indians visited our camp, bringing fish, both fresh and dried, which they exchanged for old clothes."[8]

In the later years of westward migration, however, American Indians' anger toward the settlers grew, and they did attack some wagon trains. The travelers spread some diseases, to which the Indians had never been exposed, and many died. They also killed buffalo, one of the American Indians' main food sources. Some travelers treated the Indians as animals and shot them for sport.

The Day's End

After a tiring day, travelers welcomed the sound of the trumpet blow again at 6 P.M. That meant the captain and the young men who worked as **scouts** had found a good campsite with clean water and plenty of grass for the cattle.

The desire for trade brought Native Americans and settlers together in the early westward migration.

The evening meal was a time to relax and make preparations for the next day's travel.

The captain trotted ahead and measured out a circle with stakes. Then he led as the wagons filed behind and parked in their places. The men unhitched the oxen and used the oxen's chains to attach one wagon to the next. The unbroken circle created a strong barrier against Indian attack and served as a corral for cows and horses. It also formed a common space for the travelers to do their evening chores, which helped build a strong community.

During the evening hours, the men tightened loose wagon parts or made other repairs and led the oxen out to graze. The women prepared dinner, which often was bread, bacon, and beans. But in the relaxed atmosphere of dinnertime, a woman might have more time to cook rice, buffalo, or fish. If berries grew nearby, she collected some to make a pie. She set out dough to rise overnight to bake bread in the morning. The children milked the cows, and families enjoyed fresh milk with their evening meal.

Most everyone was ready for bed by 9 P.M. Families tethered the cows and horses and set up tents within the circle for the children. Parents and babies slept in the wagon. The hired young men traveling alone slumbered on the ground under the stars.

The captain divided the men into night-watch groups. Each evening, starting at 8 P.M., members of a group were in charge of protecting the wagon circle. After a few hours on duty, they woke the next shift. All night, the men stood guard to be sure the wagons, supplies, cattle, and families were safe until morning.

Most days on the trail along the North Platte River followed the same uneventful routine, but that was only the first leg of the long journey. The travelers would miss the flat terrain once they reached more dangerous parts of the trail.

Chapter Three

Dangers and Death

Traveling the Oregon Trail was an adventure. Each day, settlers knew they were closer to a new life in Oregon. But the trail was also very dangerous. Many died along the way, and hundreds of people every year lost hope, turned back, and headed home. These "go-backs," as they were called, often had valuable information to share with future travelers, but they also shared their disappointment. People heading out on the trail knew they would face many dangers.

All travelers feared the lack of clean water. Sometimes a water source contained dangerous levels of alkali, mineral salts that could be deadly to animals and people. Many travelers learned to recognize unsafe sources when they saw dead cattle or bones scattered on the banks. Water along the trail often tasted foul, so families boiled it to make coffee. They did not know it at the time, but boiling it may have saved their lives; boiling water kills illness-causing germs.

A deadly disease called **cholera**, also spread by dirty water, was a constant threat. Cholera hit fast and hard. A victim might develop a stomachache in the morning and die by nighttime. Sometimes, entire families died

Many dangers awaited settlers traveling the Oregon Trail.

River crossings marked a dangerous part of every trip west.

from cholera. A woman named Martha Freel sent a letter back home in 1852 that read:

> First of all Francis Freel died June 4, 1852, and Marie Freel followed the 6th, next came Polly Casner who died the 9th and LaFayette Freel soon followed, he died the 10th, Elizabeth Freel . . . died the 11th, and her baby died the 17th. You see we have lost 7 persons in a few short days, all died of Cholera.[9]

Accidents also took the lives of travelers. Loaded rifles went off in wagons. Poisonous rattlesnakes bit travelers on long days of walking. Heavy wagon wheels crushed children who got in the way. Young

Catherine Sager described her own injury as she tried to jump off the wagon:

> On the afternoon of this day, in performing this feat [jumping], the hem of my dress caught on the axle-handle, precipitating me under the wheels both of which passed over me, badly crushing the left leg, before Father could stop the oxen. Seeing me clear of the wheels he picked me up. . . . A glance at my limb dangling in the air . . . he exclaimed, "My dear child, your leg is broken all to pieces!"[10]

Crossing Rivers

Crossing rivers was one of the most dangerous events of the journey. Hundreds died trying. At shallow, narrow crossings, families drove their wagons straight across. They had to watch for rocks or muddy river bottoms. If a wagon overturned, all of its contents might be ruined. The strong currents and cold waters of larger rivers drowned many travelers. The Deschutes, Columbia, and Snake Rivers of Idaho, Washington, and Oregon were especially high and rapid. The North Platte, while not very deep, had a very uneven river bottom.

Some wagons were designed with detachable wheels and watertight beds so they could be used like boats to float supplies and people across to the far bank. Animals had to swim across on their own. Amelia Stewart Knight observed others crossing a river as she waited her turn:

> There is no ferry here and the men will have to make one out of the tightest wagon-bed. . . . Everything must now be hauled out of the wagon head

over heels . . . then the wagons must be all taken to pieces, and then by means of a strong rope stretched across the river with a tight wagon-bed attached to the middle of it, the rope must be long enough to pull from one side to the other, with men on each side of the river to pull it. In this way we have to cross everything a little at a time.[11]

Some people, including Native Americans, offered river crossing services for a fee. They built ferries out of wood planks laid over canoes. They charged wagons from $1 to $16 to ride the ferry across the river. But even on a ferry, people were not always safe from rushing water.

All Kinds of Weather

Weather caused its own dangers on the trail. The dry winds and hot sun of the plains caused travelers' lips to chap and crack so that they had to use grease from the wagon wheels as lip balm. Sudden rainstorms soaked everything in the wagons and caused oxen to slip on muddy paths. During bad thunderstorms, lightning struck and killed some travelers. Everyone had to find shelter from the whipping winds of a tornado or fist-size icy hailstones.

Elizabeth Smith Geer was especially sick of bad weather. Nearing the end of the journey, she wrote in her diary:

It rains and snows. . . . I carry my babe and lead, or rather carry, another through snow, mud and water, almost to my knees. It is the worst road. . . . I went ahead with my children and I was afraid to look

Blowing snow and hail added to the misery of the long journey.

behind me for fear of seeing the wagons turn over into the mud. . . . I was so cold and numb I could not tell by feeling that I had any feet at all.[12]

Death on the Trail

When death did occur on the trail, men made coffins by carving out tree trunks or nailing together spare wagon boards. If there wasn't enough time to make a coffin or dig a hole, they just wrapped a body in a sheet and left it by the road. The graves and bodies along the trail were a sad sight for those who followed. Cecilia Adams wrote:

> *June 16, 1852* Passed eleven new graves. *June 17* Another man died near us today, and an old lady 56 years old—we passed 21 new graves It makes it seem very gloomy.[13]

A carved headstone marks the burial site of a pioneer who died on the Oregon Trail.

Some people carved messages and notes to future travelers on the bones scattered on the ground, warning of bad water at a certain stream, or offering words of encouragement.

Historians estimate that most families lost at least one member to death on the trail. But the possibility of death did not stop the travelers as they marched toward Oregon. They had known from the start that the trail would not be easy. They held on to hope for the new life waiting for them in Oregon and to the loved ones traveling with them.

Chapter Four

Keeping Hope

Life on the trail was filled with danger, and even the dullest days were hard work—walking and camping, walking and camping. But many travelers were also excited by their new experiences. They journeyed to new places and learned new things, and in small ways tried to make life on the road feel like home.

After a long day of walking, most people were very tired. But those who climbed into their tents early might hear the sounds of those who were not yet sleepy—the tune of an accordion, flute, or violin and the lighthearted steps of dancing. Some stayed up late telling stories. If company rules allowed, men sometimes played cards and gambled.

Many couples got married along the trail. Though they could not plan a fancy wedding, the travelers tried to make it a happy occasion. Jumping-off towns were popular places for weddings. If there was a pastor among the members of a wagon train, some men and women married when the company took a break. Some waited until they reached the frontier.

The custom of the time was to marry at a very young age, often early teens. Marriage was more often a

The travelers relaxed at day's end with music, dancing, storytelling, and card games.

match based on convenience and necessity for survival rather than for love. Mrs. John Kirkwood recalled:

> John Kirkwood . . . stayed at our house over night. I had met him before and when he heard the discussion about my brother's Jasper's wedding, he suggested that he and I also get married. I was nearly fifteen years old and I thought it was high time that I got married so I consented.[14]

Just as the wagon train could not stop for death or illness, it could not stop for childbirth. The birth of a baby happened often on the trail, but it could be very dangerous. Most women gave birth during a day of travel, inside the bumpy wagon. Caroline Sawyer and other women in her wagon train assisted in the birth of a baby on a stormy day in a flooded wagon. In her diary, she describes the scene: "Within a tent, during the storm, were nurses wading around a bedside placed upon chairs ministering to a mother and new-born babe."[15] Some babies born in these conditions did not survive a week, and some mothers died during childbirth. Those who stayed healthy then had to deal with the challenge of taking care of an infant while traveling.

For religious reasons, some wagon trains stopped for the whole day on Sundays. At home, Sunday was a day to go to church and to rest. But on the trail, some wagon trains treated Sunday like any other day and traveled as usual.

A woman cradles her child, one of many born on the trail.

Those wagon trains that did stop also worked. If the company included a minister, he would lead a service from the center of the corral circle. While he spoke, people went on with their chores.

Fort Laramie

After about two months crossing the plains, most travelers were thrilled to reach Fort Laramie, in what is today Wyoming. Troops manning the fort, run by the federal government, were in charge of protecting the travelers on their trip across America. Most wagon trains stopped at the fort for a few days. People bought supplies such as rice, coffee, or medicine. Men fixed

A welcome sight for weary travelers, Fort Laramie offered a place to rest and buy supplies.

their wagons. Records show that by the late 1860s, 350,000 travelers had passed through Fort Laramie.

Fort Laramie also ran a mail service. After the lonely days of travel, people were eager for news from home—for some the hardest part of the trip had been saying goodbye to family who stayed behind—and eager to mail their own stories of the trip.

Independence Rock

After Fort Laramie, many travelers looked out for a popular landmark called Independence Rock in modern-day Wyoming. It has been called the Great Register of the Desert. Adventurous travelers climbed the rock and carved out their names. They had fun searching out the names of friends or family who may have already made the trip.

Independence Rock was named by fur trappers who stopped there to celebrate Independence Day on July 4, 1825. The Oregon travelers carried on this tradition, setting a goal of reaching Independence Rock by July 4. This meant they were making good time and were likely to cross the mountains before winter.

Independence Rock was a perfect place to take a few days' rest because of the green grass surrounding the clean water of the Sweetwater River. To celebrate July 4, people unpacked their musical instruments and filled the air with patriotic songs. Men shot their guns in salute. Someone read the Declaration of Independence.

Women took the time to prepare as large a feast as possible. Men made loose boards and wagon parts into

The shores of the Sweetwater River near Independence Rock were a perfect resting place for travelers.

long tables so the company could enjoy a meal together. The women on Enoch Conyer's wagon train did something even more special: "One lady brought forth a sheet. This gave the ladies an idea. Quick as thought, another brought a skirt for the red stripes."[16] When another woman found a blue jacket in her trunk, the women sewed their own American flag, which the settlers raised proudly over camp.

Many Obstacles Remained

After a long break at Independence Rock, wagons next rolled past Devil's Gate, a deeply cut canyon, on their way to cross the Rocky Mountains. If the weather was fair, the crossing was less difficult than travelers feared. Upon going through the South Pass through the mountains, Reverend Samuel Parker wrote:

> In passing the mountains we go through a valley from five to twenty five miles wide. Some ups and downs, but comparatively speaking it is a plain so gradual in its ascent and descent . . . I should not imagine we are passing the Rocky Mountains.[17]

While crossing the Rockies seemed easy, the settlers were only a little more than halfway to their final destination, with about two or three months left and eight hundred miles to go.

Settlers hoped for fair weather as they approached the Rocky Mountains.

They stopped next at Fort Hall on the Snake River. Some of the most dangerous parts of the journey were still ahead. The banks of the Snake River were described by Cecelia Adams as a "desert of 35 miles."[18] J. T. Kerns described it "as poor country as ever; soil is sandy loam and mucky clay."[19] The land was rocky and often caused the oxens' feet to bleed.

Even though the wagon train was traveling along a river, the water of the Snake was difficult to get to. Deep cliffs plunged down the banks on either side, almost

Some parts of the Rocky Mountains were easy to cross.

Successful crossings of the Rocky Mountains were bittersweet. The settlers still had another eight hundred miles to go.

impossible for animals or wagons to get down. John McAllister wrote:

> August 19 A very rocky road hard on waggons. A watering place supposed $2\frac{1}{2}$ miles and by close observation this may be found the river has precipitous banks in places 200 feet of rock perpendicular . . .[20]

The faith that they were almost there kept the travelers going. Next, the Blue Mountains loomed in their path. While they displayed a beautiful view, they were treacherous. The hills were muddy, rocky, and slick, causing oxen to slip. Before they reached the mountains, the travelers dumped out all unnecessary belongings along the side of the trail to keep the oxens' loads light. Even so, the oxen, already growing weak, often could not pull the wagons up such steep slopes. Instead, settlers rigged the wheels of one wagon with rope on top of the hills to pull other wagons up like a large pulley. Going down such steep slopes was also difficult. Wagons sometimes rolled down too fast and crashed to pieces at the bottom. Wagons and cattle were lowered down the cliffs one by one.

Jesse Applegate remembers how earlier travelers helped those to follow by clearing the route through the mountains for settlers:

> The timber had to be cut and removed to make a way for the wagons. The trees were cut just near enough to the ground to allow the wagons to pass over the stumps, and the road through the forest was only cleared out wide enough for a wagon to pass along.[21]

After surviving the Blue Mountains, settlers had to choose whether to ride down the harsh rapids of the Columbia River or to take on the cliffs and woods of the Barlow Road. Those settlers choosing the river left their wagons behind and packed whatever was absolutely needed on their backs. They built their own boats or hired Indians to lead them down the river, camping on the banks at night. But the trip was often slowed by harsh winds and weather:

> Oct 6 We have engaged our passage down the Columbia this morning in a canoe with the Indians

Left our wagon to be shiped to order after the rush is over The wind blew so heavy that we were obliged to lay by it not being safe to travel in the canoe.[22]

Settlers who braved the Barlow Road found equal trouble. Like on the Blue Mountains, they also had to tie ropes to the wagons, and wind the ropes around trees at the top of the steep inclines. Then the men slowly lowered the wagons down. The heavy loads pulled so hard on the ropes that they cut deep grooves in the tree trunks.

A wagon train slowly climbs a steep mountain path.

On arrival in Oregon Country, settlers quickly set about building log houses and farming fertile land.

Enoch Conyers remembers a dangerous halt on the Barlow Road that almost killed one of his oxen:

> Something had happened to one of the teams ahead of us, which caused a stoppage of all the teams on the hill back of them. When our leaders stopped, and the hill being so very steep, the other oxen in the team telescoped them, caused by our wagon running onto them. In the mix-up, one of our wheel oxen had his neck so wrenched that a stream of blood . . . spurted from his nose.[23]

The travelers sometimes cut down trees and tied them to the backs of the wagons to help slow them down as they descended the dangerous slopes.

But when they arrived in the Willamette Valley in Oregon Country, most felt the trip had been worth it. The land was rich for farming. Families hurried to build log cabins that would give them shelter for the cold winter ahead, and filled their cabins with the few belongings that had survived the trip. They built corrals for their animals and planned the coming planting season. They could finally say that they were home.

Traffic on the trail was busy until the transcontinental railroad was finished in 1869. The railroad gave people a faster way to reach Oregon. But many wagon trains still took the trail until the early 1880s. People continued to journey west, all the way to the Pacific Ocean, until all of America was settled. These travelers all had hope for a better life. And the deep ruts the wagons carved into the ground across America, and into the history of this country, can still be seen today.

Notes

Chapter One: Supplying the Prairie Schooner

1. Quoted in Martin Ridge, ed., *Westward Journeys: Memoirs of Jesse A. Applegate and Lavinia Honeyman Porter Who Traveled the Overland Trail.* Chicago: R. R. Donnelley, 1989, pp. 20–21.
2. Quoted in Michael Trinklein, "All About the Trail," *The Oregon Trail,* 1999, www.isu.edu/~trinmich/ Oregontrail.html.
3. Quoted in Richard Dunlop, *Great Trails of the West.* Nashville, TN: Abingdon, 1971, p. 92.
4. Quoted in Lillian Schlissel, *Women's Diaries of the Westward Journey.* New York: Schocken, 1992, p. 170.

Chapter Two: A Day on the Dusty Trail

5. Quoted in Ridge, *Westward Journeys,* pp. 25–26.
6. Quoted in Schlissel, *Women's Diaries of the Westward Journey,* p. 173.
7. Quoted in Schlissel, *Women's Diaries of the Westward Journey,* p. 192.
8. Quoted in Ridge, *Westward Journeys,* p. 59.

Chapter Three: Dangers and Death

9. Quoted in Jim Tompkins, "The Road to Oregon," *End of the Oregon Trail,* www.endoftheoregontrail.org.

10. Quoted in Schlissel, *Women's Diaries of the Westward Journey*, p. 39.
11. Quoted in Schlissel, *Women's Diaries of the Westward Journey*, p. 204.
12. Quoted in Schlissel, *Women's Diaries of the Westward Journey*, p. 55.
13. Quoted in Todd Webb, *The Gold Rush Trail and the Road to Oregon.* Garden City, NY: Doubleday, 1963, p. 72.

Chapter Four: Keeping Hope

14. Quoted in Schlissel, *Women's Diaries of the Westward Journey*, p. 45.
15. Quoted in Schlissel, *Women's Diaries of the Westward Journey*, p. 57.
16. Quoted in Dunlop, *Great Trails of the West*, p. 127.
17. Quoted in Webb, *The Gold Rush Trail and the Road to Oregon*, p. 109.
18. Quoted in Webb, *The Gold Rush Trail and the Road to Oregon*, p. 184.
19. Quoted in Webb, *The Gold Rush Trail and the Road to Oregon*, p. 182.
20. Quoted in Webb, *The Gold Rush Trail and the Road to Oregon*, p. 182.
21. Quoted in Ridge, *Westward Journeys*, p. 72.
22. Quoted in Schlissel, *Women's Diaries of the Westward Journey*, p. 195.
23. Quoted in Dunlop, *Great Trails of the West*, p. 150.

Glossary

buffalo chips: Dried droppings from buffalo that the travelers used to start fires.

cholera: A deadly disease that hit many travelers.

jerking: A method travelers and American Indians used to cure, or dry, meat so it would last longer.

jumping-off spots: Towns where people began their journey on the Oregon Trail.

keg: A small barrel.

schooner: A large sailing ship.

scouts: Men who rode ahead of the wagon train on horseback to search for campsites.

For Further Exploration

Books

Paul Erickson, *Daily Life in a Covered Wagon*. Washington, DC: The Preservation Press, 1994. Takes readers through a day on the trail through the eyes of one family.

Judith E. Greenberg and Helen Carey McKeever, *A Pioneer Woman's Memoir*. New York: Franklin Watts, 1995. Presents the diary of Arabella Clemens Fulton and her experiences on the trail.

Jacqueline Morley, *How Would You Survive in the American West?* Danbury, CT: Franklin Watts, 1995. Covers the treacherous wagon train journey from start to finish.

Scott Steedman, *A Frontier Fort on the Oregon Trail*. New York: Peter Bedrick Books, 1993. Covers how forts were built, how they were used, and the fort's relation to American Indians and travelers on the trail.

Rebecca Stefoff, *Children of the Westward Trail*. Brookfield, CT: Millbrook Press, 1996. Discusses how difficult and adventurous a child found the westward journey.

Laura Wilson, *How I Survived the Oregon Trail: The Journal of Jesse Adams*. New York: Beech Tree Books, 1999. Each page of this book describes a different time and place on the trail as a boy and his family head to the West.

Elvira Woodruff, *Dear Levi: Letters from the Overland Trail.* New York: Alfred A. Knopf, 1994. This fictional story is told by a series of letters from a boy on the trail to his brother back home.

Websites

End of the Oregon Trail Interpretive Center
www.endoftheoregontrail.org
This website provides a history of the trail, excerpts from diaries, and information about how to visit the historic museums related to the trail.

The National Oregon/California Trail Center
www.oregontrailcenter.org
This official website offers interesting trivia, a trail map, and a timeline. Find out how to visit the Trail Center in Montpelier, Idaho and learn about its changing exhibits and activities.

Index

accidents, 22–23
Adams, Cecilia
  on graves, 25
  on Snake River, 34
animals, 8, 35
Applegate, Jesse A.
  on getting ready every
    morning, 14
  on hardships of
    journey, 7
  on Indians, 16
  on route through
    mountains, 36

Barlow Road, 36–37, 39
Big Blue River, 6
Blue Mountains, 35–37
breakfast, 13, 14
buffalo, 14–15, 17
buffalo chips, 13
Burnett, Peter, 8

cattle. *See* cows and cattle
childbirth, 28–29
children, 14, 18–19
cholera, 20, 22–23
clothes, 10, 16
Columbia River, 7, 36
companies. *See* wagon
  trains
Conyers, Enoch
  on Barlow Road, 37, 39

  on Independence Day
    at Independence
    Rock, 32
Council Bluffs, Iowa, 5
cows and cattle, 13, 14, 18,
  19

dangers
  accidents, 22–23
  diseases, 20, 22–23
  Indians, 16–17
  unsafe water, 20, 26
  weather, 12, 24–25
deaths
  from accidents, 22
  childbirth and, 29
  from diseases, 20, 22–23
  graves and, 25
Devil's Gate, 32
dinner, 18
diseases
  Indians and, 17
  wagon trains and, 20,
    22–23

entertainment, 27

food
  breakfast, 13, 14
  dinner, 18
  fresh meat, 14
  Indians and, 16

jerky, 15
    at nooning, 16
    supplies, 8–9
Fort Hall, 34
Fort Laramie, 6, 30–31
Freel, Martha, 23
fuel, 13

Geer, Elizabeth Smith,
    24–25
go-backs, 20
graves, 25
Great Migration, 4
Great Plains, 12
Great Register of the
    Desert, 31–32
guides, 12

Haun, Catherine
    on choosing members
        of company, 11
    on nooning, 16
hunting, 14–15

Independence, Missouri,
    5, 7
Independence Day, 31–32
Independence Rock, 6,
    31–32
Indians, 16–17, 24
injuries, 22–23

jerky, 15
journey
    length of, 7
    reasons for, 4–5

route of, 5–7
    time of start of, 12
July 4th, 31–32

Kerns, J. T., 34
Kirkwood, Mrs. John, 28
Knight, Amelia Stewart,
    23–24

leaders, 12

mail, 31
marriages, 27–28
McAllister, John, 34–35
men, work of
    during evening, 18
    as hunters, 14–15
    as night watchmen, 13,
        19
    as scouts, 17
missionaries, 5

Native Americans, 16–17,
    24
nooning, 16
North Platte River, 6, 13,
    23–24

Oregon-California Trail, 5
Oregon Country
    arrival in, 39
    described, 4, 7
Oregon Trail, 5–7

Palmer, Joel, 9
Panic of 1837, 4
Parker, Samuel, 33

pastors
    importance of, 11
    marriages and, 27
    Sunday services and, 30
prairie schooners, 8

railroad, 39
rivers
    Big Blue, 6
    Columbia, 7, 36
    crossing, 23 24, 37
    importance of, 6
    North Platte, 6, 13,
        23–24
    Snake, 6, 34
    Sweetwater, 6, 31
Rocky Mountains
    crossing, 6, 32 33
    winter in, 12
Rudd, Lydia Allen, 16

Sager, Catherine, 23
Sawyer, Caroline, 28–29
schooners, 8
scouts, 17
slavery, 4–5
Snake River, 6, 34
St. Joseph, Missouri, 5
Sundays, 29–30
supplies, 10
    animals, 8
    cost of, 7

food, 8–9
    at Fort Laramie, 30–31
    see also wagons
Sweetwater River, 6, 31

towns, jumping-off, 5, 7,
    27
trade, 16
transcontinental railroad,
    39

wagons
    described, 7–8, 23
    leaving behind, 36
    steep slopes and, 35–36,
        37
wagon trains
    getting ready in morn-
        ing, 14
    members of, 10–12, 27,
        30
    order of wagons in, 14
    parking at night, 17–18
    size of, 12
walking, 16
water
    safe, 31
    unsafe, 20, 26
weather, 12, 24–25
Willamette Valley, 7, 39
women, work of, 13, 18
Wyoming, 30–32

Picture Credits